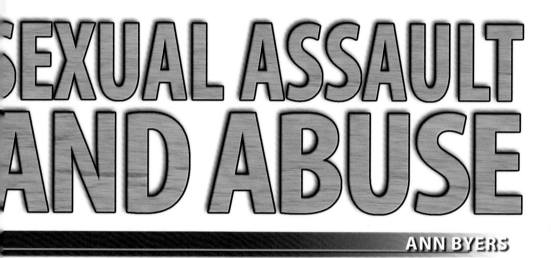

# SEXUAL ASSAULT AND ABUSE

ANN BYERS

ROSEN
PUBLISHING®

New York

Published in 2016 by The Rosen Publishing Group, Inc.
29 East 21st Street, New York, NY 10010

First Edition

**Library of Congress Cataloging in Publication Data**

Byers, Ann.
Sexual assault and abuse / Ann Byers. – First edition.
    pages cm. – (Confronting violence against women)
Includes bibliographical references and index.
ISBN 978-1-4994-6042-1 (library bound) – ISBN 978-1-4994-6043-8 (pbk.)
– ISBN 978-1-4994-6044-5 (6-pack)
1.  Sex crimes–Juvenile literature. 2.  Child sexual abuse–Juvenile literature.
3.  Women–Violence against–Juvenile literature. 4.  Women–Crimes against-
-Juvenile literature.  I. Title.
 HV6556.B94 2016
 364.15'3–dc23
                                                                2014048787

*Manufactured in the United States of America*

# CONTENTS

# INTRODUCTION

Tiffany had no reason to fear her boss. They went to the same church and she had known him for years. When he offered her a job at his bookstore, she jumped at the chance. At sixteen, she wanted to buy a car, and this job would help her afford it. But when he started asking personal questions, she felt uncomfortable. She was really surprised when he asked, "Tiffany, are you a virgin?" He complimented her on her decision to wait until marriage, and she decided he was just being friendly. Still, the comment bothered her.

A few days later, when he asked if she had a boyfriend, she felt that uncomfortable twinge again. In the days and weeks that followed, when her boss told her she was pretty or smart or talented, she felt awkward. But she was also flattered that a nice–looking man in his thirties noticed her. It was all very confusing.

One day her brother, who was her means of transportation, had to work late. Her boss offered to give her a ride home. She thought nothing of it until he said, "Let's stop at my place." He had some books to show her. The uncomfortable feeling returned, but she reasoned it away. He had never done anything to her, and he was her boss. She liked her job. So she agreed.

At his house, he kissed her gently and led her to his bedroom. Later she said, "I didn't want it to happen. But at the same time, it seemed inevitable." She was too mixed up and frightened to do

Sexually suggestive words and looks sometimes lead to harassing touches and actions. If someone's behavior makes you feel uncomfortable, say something.

anything but follow his lead. She felt trapped. And she thought it was all her fault.

After that day, Tiffany's boss gave her many rides home. Once, when she thought she might be pregnant, she was stunned by his cold, selfish, and cruel response. For a year, she lived not only with the sex, but also with anger, self-hatred, and shame. She kept the truth hidden from her parents, her brother, and everyone else.

Many years later, she poured out her hurt to a counselor. The counselor helped her see that her boss had taken advantage of her and that she was not to blame. After many counselling sessions, she found peace and healing and was able to put the painful ordeal behind her. Now she shares her experience as a way to help and warn others about sexual predators.

Tiffany's story, which she told under an assumed name to *Christianity Today*, illustrates some common themes in the ugly picture of sexual violence. For one, predators are very seldom strangers; they are usually people the victim knows and trusts. Their assaults are not spontaneous acts, but are carefully planned. The predator does not love the victim; he uses her. And he leaves her with deep and undeserved guilt and humiliation.

Like Tiffany, many victims of sexual abuse are reluctant to tell anyone about their secret nightmare. But seeking help and talking with a trusted person are the first steps toward healing. This resource was written so people will know that help is available. It was written so that victims can overcome the violence and abuse they experienced and move from victim to survivor.

# CHAPTER 1

# The Many Forms of Sexual Violence

Sadly, Tiffany's story is not rare. The Centers for Disease Control and Prevention (CDC) reports that almost one in five women in the United States has been raped at some point in her life. The Rape, Abuse, and Incest National Network (RAINN) estimates that a sexual assault occurs once every two minutes. That makes sexual assault one of the biggest categories of crime in the United States.

The U.S. Department of Justice defines the crime of sexual assault as "any type of sexual contact or behavior that occurs without the explicit consent of the recipient." Let's take that definition apart. It has three components: sexual contact, sexual behavior, and "without explicit consent."

## Sexual Contact and Sexual Behavior

Sexual contact occurs when a person touches the sexual areas of another person. That means anything around the private parts and the breasts. Obviously intercourse—having sex—is sexual contact. So is fondling, or intentionally rubbing, private body parts. To meet the definition, the contact does not have to be skin to skin; if one person touches another sexually through clothes, the touching is

Spying on people while they are undressing may seem harmless, but it uses other people to satisfy the viewer's personal desires. It robs victims of their right to privacy.

sexual contact. If done without consent rape, oral and anal sex, and fondling are crimes.

Sexual behavior encompasses actions that do not necessarily involve physical contact. Actions that make people feel good sexually are sexual behaviors even if there is no physical touch. When those actions involve other people without their consent, they are forms of sexual assault.

One example of noncontact sexual behavior is voyeurism. Voyeurs are "peeping Toms"; they seek sexual enjoyment from looking at a naked or partially undressed person or watching people engaged in sexual activity. They might peep secretly, without letting the other person know they are looking, or they might force or persuade their victim to "perform" for them. Either way, the behavior is criminal.

The flip side of voyeurism is exhibitionism. Instead of looking at others, exhibitionists want others to look at them. They get sexual pleasure by exposing themselves, either completely naked or uncovering private parts. Exhibitionism is also called flashing or indecent exposure. Most exhibitionists do not actually want physical contact with their victims. They are satisfied with the shocked reactions to their behavior. Exhibitionism is often a misdemeanor (a minor crime), but it is still a crime.

Other noncontact sexual behaviors involve pornography. Pornography is the depiction of sexual behavior for the primary purpose of arousing sexual interest. It could be a photograph, a video, or a text. Merely possessing pornography is not necessarily illegal. However, both possessing and distributing pornography become sexual assault, and therefore criminal, when the pictures are of children or are taken without consent.

# Explicit Consent

The common thread in all these behaviors, and part of the definition of sexual assault, is that the actions are taken without the explicit consent of the recipient. Of course if any force is involved, the action is obviously without the victim's consent. But the absence of force does not mean the victim consented. For the action not to be assault, consent must be explicit. That means the recipient of the

Revealing fashions may make girls feel flirty and might make boys want to look. But they are not an invitation or an excuse for sex.

action has to say "yes" very clearly, without any question. Not saying "no" is not the same thing as saying "yes."

Sometimes victims cannot say "no." They may be paralyzed by fear and unable to say or do anything to stop the assault. They may be caught off guard and confused so they cannot understand what is happening to them or figure out what to do about it. If they have been drinking or taking drugs, they may be physically and mentally unable to say "no"; their thinking is very likely muddled and their reactions stalled.

Some assaulters apply psychological pressure to make their victims believe they are agreeing to the sex. A man may tell a girl she obviously wanted sex because she flirted with him or dressed in a sexy way. He might try to convince her that she needs to have sex with him to prove she loves him. He may say she owes him sex because of something he did for her. If she said "yes" to him before, he might try to make her think she can never tell him "no." None of these statements are true. Flirting, loving someone, being grateful, and saying "yes" previously are not expressions of consent.

Consent must not only be explicit for an act not to be assault, but it must also be legal. Some states have ruled that a person who is intoxicated is not legally able to give consent. Two categories of people cannot legally consent to sex: those who are mentally or developmentally impaired and minors, or those under the age of adulthood. Depending on the state, the age of consent is sixteen, seventeen, or eighteen. In Canada, the age of consent for sexual activity is sixteen years unless the activity exploits the child, in which case the age of consent is eighteen. This means that even if young people say "yes" to having sex, they may not be able to say "yes" legally, and an adult who has sex with them may be guilty of sexual assault.

# MYTHS and *FACTS*

**MYTH** If a person does not say "no" or fight back, it is not sexual assault.

**Victims do not fight back for a number of reasons. If explicit consent is not given, it is sexual assault.**

**MYTH** Women sometimes are partly responsible for sexual assaults if they dress or act in sexy ways.

**The person who commits the assault is totally responsible.**

**MYTH** Sex is not rape if two people have had consensual sex in the past.

**Any time a person does not consent to sex and another insists, it is rape.**

# The Scope of the Issue

How big is the problem of sexual assault? In terms of the number of people affected, it is huge. According to the U.S. Bureau of Justice Statistics, there were 346,830 sexual assaults of people over the age of twelve in 2012. That figure does not take into account the sexual violence against children. The CDC estimates that one in four girls and one in six boys in the United States are sexually abused before their eighteenth birthday. Nearly everyone knows someone who has been assaulted sexually.

Even though every form of sexual assault is a crime, more than half of all victims do not report what happened. Some are so

Sexual assault is sometimes called a lonely crime because many victims are too shocked, sad, or embarrassed to admit it happened to them. Many suffer alone, in silence.

embarrassed at the invasion of something so private and personal that they do not want to have to talk to anyone about the incident. Some are afraid they will be in trouble for being somewhere they shouldn't have been or doing something they shouldn't have done. Others are concerned the assaulter will do something to get back at them if they tell.

Many victims do not report the crime because they are afraid of the response they might receive. What if the police do not believe them? What if the assaulter says they consented; how can they prove they didn't? Maybe their friends will think it is not really a big deal.

Worst of all is the nagging doubt most victims feel that it was really their fault, at least in part. If I weren't walking by myself … If I hadn't gone to that party … If I hadn't smiled when he looked at me … If I had just screamed … If I hadn't had anything to drink … If I hadn't let him kiss me … Most victims find some reason to blame themselves.

# Know the Facts

But the truth is, no victim is to blame for an assault, not even a little. Many sexual assaulters are master manipulators. They are very good at confusing their victims into thinking they are somehow responsible for the attack or the abuse. A young man tells his date, "You are so hot I can't help myself," and she thinks his actions are her fault. An adult tells a child, "I'm doing this because I love you," and the child thinks she is to blame for what the adult did to her. A girl gets drunk, wakes up naked, and believes she deserved whatever happened to her. But no matter what the attacker or abuser says, the attacker is the one at fault.

Attacks are most often committed by someone known to the victim. They know how to charm and gain the trust of the victim.

One of the reasons victims so easily blame themselves is that they know and often like their attackers. Fewer than 14 percent of sexual assaults are perpetrated by strangers. They are usually committed by friends, neighbors, family members, boyfriends or girlfriends, and other acquaintances of the victims. These people can be charmers, cultivating the trust of their victims before they attack. Their victims, especially children, have a hard time believing someone they trust would hurt them; so they blame themselves.

There is no profile of a typical sexual assaulter. Offenders can be male or female, although the overwhelming majority are male. Both genders are assaulted, but women and girls are victims far more often than men and boys. Offenders can be almost any age, from elderly to teenage or preteen. Their motivation is sometimes to satisfy their sexual feelings, but more often sexual violence is an attempt to feel powerful by controlling another person. Sexual assaulters look for someone who appears less strong than they. They may be able to manipulate someone they know or use force on a stranger. Sadly, some choose to victimize children

# CHAPTER 2

# Sexual Violence Against Children

Child sexual abuse is any sexual behavior an older person does with a child—touching, showing, or looking. No one knows exactly how common child sexual abuse is. Many children who are assaulted do not tell anyone until years after the fact, if then.

The terms "sexual abuse" and "sexual assault" are often used to mean the same thing. But the word "abuse" adds the additional element that the assaulter took advantage of, or abused, some position he or she had over the person assaulted. Abusers usually have some power over their victims that cause the victims to respect, need, or trust them. The power might be age, size, or position of authority. Taking advantage of that position to manipulate a child into any kind of sexual contact or behavior is sexual abuse. It may be a single assault or it may be a series of events that go on for months or years.

## The Vocabulary of Child Abuse

The different words people use when they talk about child abuse can be confusing. The word most often used to refer to sexual abuse

Sexual predators who are pedophiles often look for children who are alone. They might hang out in or near places children go, such as schools, arcades, parks, and playgrounds.

is "molestation." The terms "molester" and "offender" mean the same thing. A child molester is someone who bothers, or molests, a child in any sexual way. An offender is someone who commits an offense—a criminal act—of any kind.

A predator is a particular type of abuser. Just as an animal predator hunts for prey, a sexual predator searches for people to assault. Predators often look for specific kinds of children, maybe children of a certain race or a particular age range. Because children grow out of the age category they prefer, predators are very often repeat offenders. That is, they are serial abusers, assaulting more than one victim. When a child becomes older than they like, they hunt for new prey. That is also the reason they frequently take pictures of the children they abuse.

A term specific to child abuse is pedophilia. Pedophilia is interest in children, particularly children who have not yet reached puberty, as sexual objects. Although pedophiles are attracted to children, many also have normal sex lives with people their own age. Pedophilia is not an act or an offense; it is a way of thinking. Psychologists classify pedophilia as a mental disorder. Because pedophilia is a mental condition, a pedophile is usually a pedophile for life. Some pedophiles receive help and control their disorder, never committing any sexual crime. Many others, however, become sexual predators.

## Sex Crimes Against Children

Any form of child molestation is a crime. One very specific sex crime against children is incest. Definitions differ slightly, but generally incest is sexual violation by someone closely related. In some states, closely related means by blood and in some states stepparents and stepsiblings are also considered close relatives. In some places, any form of sexual contact between such parties is classified as incest; in others, only actual intercourse qualifies. The reason for the distinction is that some states have different laws and penalties for incest and for other forms of child sexual abuse.

Separate laws also govern the crime of sexual exploitation. Sexual exploitation is abusing children sexually for personal, most often financial, gain. That usually means making a child a prostitute (also called sex trafficking) or using a child to produce pornography.

These demonstrators are protesting a website that is engaged in sex trafficking. The website lures young women with the promise of a job or a relationship and then sells them into prostitution.

Another very specific sex crime against children is statutory rape. Rape means that intercourse, or actual sexual penetration, has taken place. Statutory rape is rape of a person who is not able to give consent according to the law, or statute. That usually means someone under the legal age of consent. That age ranges from sixteen in some states to eighteen in others. Children can be charged with statutory rape if there is a significant age difference between the offending child and the child raped, sometimes as few as three years. Remember: an underage person cannot legally give consent, and any sex partner of that person may be guilty of statutory rape.

It is not always easy to tell a person's age. If this girl is underage, up to eighteen in some states, she cannot give explicit consent and her boyfriend can be charged with statutory rape even if she agrees to sex.

## Keeping Silent

Who commits these crimes against the most vulnerable in the population? According to a Bureau of Justice Statistics 2000 report, about a third of child sexual abuse is perpetrated by family members, 7 percent by strangers, and nearly 60 percent by non-family members the child knows. Child molesters might be neighbors, babysitters, teachers, coaches, or family friends.

# A PROMISE

They were both on family vacations, staying in cabins next door to each other. She was thirteen; he was sixteen. She didn't say the word "no", but she cried and she said "stop" over and over. But he didn't stop; he raped her. It was just once, but it was horrible. The terror of that incident never left her. She vowed she would do everything in her power so that nothing like what she experienced would ever happen to her little sister.

Sasha was never the same after that single encounter. For years she carried feelings of guilt and shame. Eventually, she got connected with a sexual assault program. The counselors there helped her understand that what was done to her was not her fault. It was a violation, an attack, a terrible crime. That realization was the beginning of her healing.

She was finally able to keep the promise she had made at age thirteen. She went to college and became a social worker, specifically helping rape victims. She is no longer a victim; she is a healer.

Even though children can name the person who assaults them, they seldom do. Even older children are reluctant to admit they have been abused. One reason is fear. Because child abusers are so good at manipulating children's thoughts and feelings, the victims often think—absolutely incorrectly!—that the abuse is their fault. So they do not tell their parents. They are afraid their parents will be angry at them, not believe them, or take the side of the abuser.

Sometimes they have reason to fear physical harm to themselves or someone they care about. The abuser may have warned them: "If you tell, I'll give you something to really cry about." "I'll hurt your mother." "I'll do the same thing to your little sister." "I'll kill your dog." Even if there is no actual threat, children often fear that if the abuser knows they told, the abuser will get back at them by doing something worse.

In more than 90 percent of child sexual violence, children have some relationship with the offender. That relationship makes telling their story difficult. Telling will probably get the abuser in trouble, and children do not want to cause problems. Sometimes they just don't know whom to tell. What do you do if the person who is supposed to protect you is molesting you? If your own brother or grandfather hurts you, whom can you trust?

Older children often fear long-term consequences. If I tell, will Mom and Dad split up? If so, where will I go? Will Child Protective Services put me with a foster family or in a group home? Will I be separated from my brothers and sisters? Teenagers may worry about what their friends or future partners will think of them if they find out what happened.

# Report Child Abuse

No matter what children fear or feel, they need to tell. If they cannot tell their parents, they should find another adult to tell—a relative,

Children who have been molested are often too frightened or confused to talk about the abuse. Adults who are gentle and patient can help them open up.

teacher, counselor, or religious or club leader. Certain adults, usu-ally those who work with children or youth, are required (mandated) by law to report anytime they hear anything about possible abuse. These mandated reporters have to tell police or child welfare agen-cies if they know of or suspect children are being sexually mistreated.

Telling what happened is important not only to stop the abuse, but also so the child can begin to overcome the consequences. The consequences of child sexual violence are many and deep. Abuse does not always leave physical injuries because the offenders often use charm rather than force to get their victims to do what they want. But the emotional damage can be seen in flashbacks, anger, depression, and low self-esteem. Many child abuse victims have a very hard time trusting people. They have difficulty forming friendships. Because they were introduced to sex in a very confusing and traumatic way, they struggle with healthy sexual relationships when they become adults.

The damage lingers years and even decades after the abuse has ended. It lasts until victims are able to see the events for the abuse they were and untangle the truth, the lies, and the emotions involved. Trained counselors and support groups can help people deal with and overcome the effects of childhood sexual violence. But in order to get this help, victims have to tell someone, no matter how long ago the abuse took place. Telling someone is hard when the ability to trust others has been badly shattered. But being brave enough to speak up is the first step toward healing.

# CHAPTER 3

# Electronic Sexual Abuse

The modern age has created a new venue for sexual violence: the Internet. The digital world is the ideal place for predators to find victims. Millions of children and youth are surfing the Web at any given time. The FBI estimates that more than half a million pedophiles are online every day. There are two types of Internet sexual predators. One type is looking for pornography. The other is hunting for people he can molest offline.

## Grooming Victims

Online predators hunt their prey carefully. They go to websites children and teens are likely to frequent. They look for screen names that appear to be created by young people—"NumberOneCheerleader" or "HelloKitty" rather than "Supermom." Sexy names like "PartyGirl" or "YoungAndWild" are even better. Predators scan online profiles and read posts.

When predators find potential victims, they create false identities. Sometimes they pretend to be younger than they are, about the same age as their intended victims. They lure their targets into a relationship with attention, sympathy, and supposed affection. They gain their trust and wait for an opportunity to strike. Police call this process "grooming."

Young people may be surprised to discover whom they have been chatting with online. This man might have posed as someone much younger for a long time before revealing his true identity.

They make their first contact through instant messaging, chat rooms, e-mail, social networking sites, or gaming forums. It is not unusual for strangers to appear on these sites, so the initial contact may not arouse suspicion. The conversation frequently begins with a comment on something the targeted child posted: "Hey, I went to that concert, too. Did you like the last song?" Predators want victims to think they share the same interests or experiences.

# Moving Offline

The chats continue for as long as it takes for the predator to gain the victim's trust and friendship. Then he steers the discussion to sexual subjects. The talk might seem innocent at first: "Do you like romantic movies?" But it progresses gradually to intimate topics: "Do you kiss on the first date?" "Are you a virgin?" "Do you like oral sex?"

These kinds of questions are called sexual solicitations. They are invitations to talk about sexual matters. Most sexual solicitations young people receive online come from their friends, not from predators. Even if they come from predators, most teens simply stop contact with the people who send them.

But some teens are charmed by predators' attentions. About 4 percent of online sexual solicitations are aggressive, which means the solicitor asks for offline contact. Some victims agree to an in-person meeting. Whether or not the victim agrees to meet, merely asking the minor to engage in sexual activity is a crime. According to federal law, using the Internet "to entice or coerce someone younger than 18 years of age to engage in sexual activity is a crime punishable by fine and not less than 10 years imprisonment."

# Online Pornography

Most electronic sexual enticement is not for offline meeting but for online pictures. The majority of Internet predators are looking for pornography. They find and groom victims, introduce sex into their discussions, and then ask for photos or videos. They want victims to send the pictures to them or to post them online. They might try to get the victim to use a webcam or a cell phone camera to record themselves nude or engaging in some sexual activity. Some predators hack into the targeted child's computer with a virus that turns

The innocent, fun picture this girl is taking might be seen by thousands of people. If she just texts it to the other girl's phone, hackers can find it and repost it hundreds of times.

on the webcam. They can see their victims without the victims realizing they are being watched.

Predators often want pictures that are more and more explicit. After receiving the first few pictures, they may bully their victims into sending more. They might threaten to post the photos, send them to the victims' friends, tell their parents, or come to their homes. People who exchange child pornography share the images in their Internet communities, chat rooms, message boards, and other places. A single image is probably viewed hundreds or even thousands of times by as many people. Thus the exploitation of the child continues long after the picture is snapped.

# A LONG WALK HOME

Everything about freshman year in college was wonderful to Salamishah Tillet. Until the night she was raped by a senior she was dating. That was when her entire life fell apart. She didn't tell anyone. Two years later, still experiencing flashbacks, she was raped a second time. More flashbacks, now with nightmares and shaking. This time she told. She told a therapist, who helped her overcome the post-traumatic stress. She told her sister, who cried with her as she struggled to regain control over her life. She told classmates in a story she wrote for a campus newspaper. In the twenty years since she was assaulted at age seventeen, she has told countless women not only the ugliness of rape but also the power of healing. With her sister, Scheherazade, she began A Long Walk Home, a nonprofit that uses the visual and performing arts to raise awareness and promote healing for women who have experienced sexual violence. She has received numerous awards for her work. Salamishah has helped many make the same long walk.

## Sexting

Most of the sexual images that wind up on the Internet today were not taken secretly with a webcam. They were not obtained by threats or manipulation from predators. Many were sent willingly by people who wanted to share them. Today, practically anyone with a cell phone can take a picture of himself or herself and text it to another person.

Sexting is dangerous business. Although there are apps that destroy texted photos after they are viewed, there are even newer apps that take screenshots of the photos and preserve them. Anything sent digitally is permanently available.

Sending sexually explicit photos by text, often called sexting, may seem harmless. You send a picture you want to send to someone who wants to get it. What could be the harm in that? Actually, several things can go wrong. What if the person you text decides to share the picture with another person or several people? What if one of those people puts it online for the whole world to see? This very scenario has led to embarrassment, teasing, and bullying.

In some schools this practice has mushroomed into sexting rings. Typically, girls send revealing images to boyfriends and the boys trade or share the pictures with their friends. One picture texted to one person can make its way to dozens of phones, scores of social media sites, and hundreds of web pages.

Having a private picture on public display is embarrassing enough, and sometimes the person's name, address, and other identifying information are posted with the picture. Boyfriends and girlfriends get mad at each other and post the sexts as a way to hurt the other. This is sometimes called revenge porn, and there are entire websites devoted to displaying these photos. Revenge porn sometimes leads to sextortion, a kind of sexual blackmail. The extortionists use the sexts to obtain money or more explicit photos.

The damage from sexting goes far beyond embarrassment. If the picture is of a person under the age of eighteen, the sender of the sext may be guilty of distributing child pornography, and the recipient may be guilty of possessing pornography. If prosecuted, the parties could be fined, be jailed, and have to register as sex offenders for the rest of their lives. The offense could become part of their permanent record, giving them a criminal history that will surface every time they apply for a scholarship or a job. People may engage in sexting as harmless flirtation, but it can have very serious consequences.

# Protecting Yourself from Electronic Abuse

To take advantage of the benefits the cyberworld has to offer while keeping yourself safe from its dangers, follow these guidelines:

• Choose a screen name that has no identifying information. It should not reveal your age or your gender. Above all, do not make it sexually suggestive.

- Do not post anything someone can use to find you. Don't mention your school or where you work. Don't talk about where you go at certain times.
- Do not fill out an online profile. Your friends already know enough about you, and strangers don't need to know anything.
- Do not post or text sexual pictures! If friends ask for sexts, respond with something funny (like a nude baby picture) or something brief and clear ("I don't do that. Period.").
- Do not open e-mails or respond to instant messages from anyone you don't know.
- If someone is harassing or soliciting you online, keep a copy of the messages. These may be helpful in finding or prosecuting the predator.
- Report any and all online solicitations to the Internet site, local law enforcement or the FBI, and to CyberTipline (www.cybertipline.com). These companies and agencies will investigate your complaint, tell you what to do, and take action against offenders.

# CHAPTER 4

# Sexual Violence in Relationships

**W**hen women hear the term "sexual violence", most think of rape. They picture an unknown man lurking in some dark place, waiting to leap out and grab them. That scene is a reality, but it is not the norm. According to the CDC, fewer than 14 percent of rapists are strangers. That means that before the assault, most victims had some relationship with their attackers.

The vast majority of rapes are acquaintance rapes. An acquaintance rape can occur on a date, at a party, in a non-dating encounter, or between intimate partners. Date rape is a serious problem today, particularly on college campuses.

## Dating Expectations

Two people who go out together often have different ideas of what should happen on a date. Some men expect to "score," or have sex, with their dates; many women want to have a good time without sex. Men sometimes think that if they spend money on their dates, the women owe them sex in return. Most women, on the other hand, believe their dates are supposed to pay and should be satisfied with a nice evening. If the two have had sex before, he may

Talking about dating expectations before going out can avoid uncomfortable situations. Thinking and planning ahead gives you some measure of mental and emotional control.

think she is willing or even wants to have sex any time they can. Or he may think she has no right to tell him "no."

Let's be clear on the facts. You never owe someone sex. Spending money on you or doing anything else for you does not give anyone the right to demand sex from you. Having sex with someone one time or many times does not mean you are obligated to have sex with him again. Even being married does not give a person the right to demand sex from you. No one but you is in charge of your body.

Sometimes women are comfortable with hugging and kissing but don't want to go any further. Their dates should not assume that a "yes" to any sexual touching is an invitation to "go all the way." Anything short of "yes" all the way to the end of the sexual encounter is "no." If she says, "Stop," that is "no." If she says nothing but tries to push away, that is "no." If she is too drunk, drugged, or afraid to resist, that is "no." Even if she says "yes" at first and then changes her mind and asks him to stop, that is also "no." Some men think their dates want them to be forceful, that her "no" really means "yes." Not true; unless consent is explicit, the sex is rape.

## Alcohol and Drugs

One thing that affects consent is the use of alcohol or drugs. These substances muddle your thinking and dull your ability to make good decisions. They can relax you physically so that it is hard to fight off a sexual attack.

Among these are substances commonly called date rate drugs. As the name implies, they are used purposely to make date rape easier. A large portion of date rapes are planned. Some men who go to parties with the intention of having sex slip drugs into their dates' drinks. Strong drugs with street names like roofies, liquid ecstasy, and Special K confuse the dates and make them physically weak. Often they pass out completely. When they come to, they are usually completely unaware that they were raped while they were out. These drugs work fast and give the men who plan date rapes total control over their victims.

But the most popular date rape "drug" is alcohol. It may take longer, but alcohol can have the same effects: confusion and loss of judgment, control, and memory. One of the problems with mixing alcohol or drugs with dating is misplacing blame. Victims often reason this way: I couldn't stop the rape because I got drunk; it's

Giving a girl a date rape drug is usually not as obvious as it appears in this picture. The best way to avoid date rape is to stay alert and pay close attention.

my fault I got drunk; therefore I'm to blame for the rape. The truth is: the victim may be at fault for drinking but being drunk is not the cause of any rape. A man's assault of a woman is his decision, his act, his fault. Drinking may have made the victim unable to resist the attack, but lack of resistance is not consent. A person under the influence of drugs or alcohol is physically and legally unable to consent to sex. No matter how she got under the influence, the person who takes advantage of her condition is the one, and the only one, to blame.

Following a person is only one form of stalking. Most stalkers use more than one method, such as sending messages, destroying property, and contacting friends.

## Stalking

Another form of sexual violence that occurs in relationships is stalking. It generally occurs in relationships that are not healthy, often after one person in the relationship has rejected the other. It is sometimes seen with former intimate partners or with a person who has an obsessive interest in someone who does not return that interest. The CDC reported that in 2010, one in six women was stalked.

Stalking is defined as at least two different types of harassment on at least two different occasions that make the victim afraid of being harmed. Harassment that is conducted online is called cyberstalking.

The stalker tries to contact his victim. He might call, text, or send messages. He might leave notes under a door or on a car. But the victim does not want to be contacted. As attempts at contact are ignored, the stalker might insert threats into the messages and deliver them through mutual friends. Stalkers often threaten to hurt not only the victim but also her relatives, pets, or friends.

Frustrated by the rejection, the stalker often follows his victim, watching and waiting for her. He may lurk outside her home, follow her online, or show up at her school or workplace. He might try to win her affection by leaving her gifts. Or he might attempt to punish her by spreading ugly rumors, creating fake web pages in her name, or vandalizing her property. Stalking and cyberstalking frequently lead to physical violence.

# Confronting Rape and Harassment

You may not be able to avoid every threat of rape and harassment, but there are measures you can take that will protect you from many. Protect yourself from date rape by not allowing yourself to be alone with an acquaintance, especially when you are just getting to know each other. Meet in public places. At parties, stay in rooms where there are several other people. Cars are prime places for date rape, so you might want to arrange your own transportation.

How do you protect yourself from date rape substances? The simple solution might seem to be stay sober. Yes, but date rape drugs can be dropped into a soda just as easily as into an alcoholic drink. So be careful about all drinking. Get your drinks yourself. Watch the bottle being opened and the drink being prepared. If you are not sure about the people giving the party, don't ladle punch

The best way to stay safe when socializing is to be in a group of people you know in a public place that sees plenty of foot traffic.

from an open punch bowl. Keep your drink where you can see it at all times.

What about the danger of stranger rape? You are less likely to be a victim if you stay away from isolated areas. If you walk or run to keep fit, exercise in places with lots of people. Pay attention to your surroundings. Change your routines; don't go the same way to the same place every day. Keep your cell phone with you, and keep it charged.

If you are being harassed, report it to the police; stalking is a crime. Keep a log of the stalker's actions and a copy of any communication from him. He may see you as a target and treat you as a victim, but you can confront the violence and take control of the situation.

# 10 GREAT QUESTIONS TO ASK
## WHEN YOU'RE ASKING FOR HELP

1. Will my parents find out I was sexually assaulted?

2. What can I do if I don't remember what happened?

3. Could I be pregnant or get an STI from the assault?

4. Where can I get a medical exam?

5. What happens in a medical exam? Who gives it?

6. Do I have to make a police report?

7. What will happen to the attacker if I report the assault?

8. What will happen if I report it and people don't believe me?

9. The assaulter lives with me, and I am afraid to go home. What should I do?

10. Are there any support groups that can help me?

# CHAPTER 5

# If It Happens

Sexual violence may be a one-time event or ongoing abuse. Either way, the effects are deep and long lasting. Assaults can inflict physical injuries, result in pregnancy, and leave sexually transmitted infections (STIs). The emotional reactions can include shock,

The effects of sexual assault do not simply go away with time. Resources are available, however, to help victims overcome them and regain control of their lives.

confusion, misplaced guilt, fear, mistrust, embarrassment, and shame. The psychological impacts very often remain for years. Sexual assault victims suffer flashbacks, post-traumatic stress disorder (PTSD), depression, and problems concentrating and sleeping. Many develop eating disorders and substance abuse, and some cut themselves or harm their bodies in other ways. Low self-esteem is common as is difficulty forming healthy relationships.

As severe as the consequences can be, they do not have to control people. With help, victims can take charge of their lives. If you or someone you know is or becomes a victim of sexual assault or sexual abuse, help is available for dealing with the immediate situation and the longer-term effects.

# Immediately Afterward

If you are assaulted, the first thing to do is get to a safe place away from the attacker. Call 911. Tell someone. Call or go to someone you trust and feel safe with and tell that person what happened. Talking with a parent, a friend, or a counselor will help you sort through the trauma and the emotions and enable you to think more clearly. If you can't think of anyone to talk to, call a rape crisis center or the national sexual assault hotline, (800) 656-HOPE. Even if you have a friend to help you, call a crisis center or hotline. A trained counselor will give you advice on what to do. Some counseling centers have advocates who will go with you as you take the next steps.

Go to an emergency room or a hospital. Rape does not always cause injuries you can see, but doctors will examine you for internal injuries. They will test for STIs. Some hospitals have nurses specially trained in examining rape victims. They will gather evidence that can be used if you or the district attorney decides to prosecute the assaulter. Many use a rape kit that has equipment for collecting

Recovering from sexual assault begins with telling someone what happened. Many hotline counselors were victims themselves, and they understand the feelings and fears of callers.

and storing samples of hair, blood, urine, and other body secretions. They are looking for the offender's DNA.

You need to preserve as much physical evidence as possible, so don't wash or change your clothes before going to the hospital. Most rape victims want to shower over and over again; don't do it yet. Don't brush your teeth or comb your hair. Try to keep from urinating before getting medical attention. Don't clean up or move anything where the attack took place; it is a crime scene.

# AN ANGRY COVER GIRL

No one would call it "rape." He was her date, not a stranger, so how could it be rape? She couldn't prove she resisted, so it was her word against his. She didn't go to a doctor right away, and when she finally went to one on campus, the health center didn't have a rape kit. The attorney she tried to hire said there was no physical evidence to support the charge of rape. The dean said the two of them should try to work things out. In 1990, the concept of date rape did not exist.

But when Katie Koestner learned that the man who had raped her assaulted another student, she decided to tell her story. It eventually appeared in *Time* magazine (she was on the June 3, 1991, cover) and on *The Oprah Winfrey Show*. The story brought the ugly reality of date rape on college campuses to light and made Koestner an activist. Since then she has spoken to thousands about sexual assault and

*continued on next page*

*continued from previous page*

Since the first Take Back the Night events in the 1970s, thousands of rallies have been held across the country. Many are in October, which is National Domestic Violence Awareness month.

helped write laws that require colleges to report the crime of rape. She is the director of the Take Back the Night Foundation, an international organization committed to ending sexual violence.

## The Police and the Courts

Rape is a serious crime. Even if you successfully fought off the attacker or he was scared away before he could finish, attempted rape is just as serious a crime. You do not have to report the assault, but if you are a minor and you go to a hospital, the doctors and nurses are required by law to inform the authorities. Even if you don't think you want to report the rape, it is a good idea to have the medical exam. Some people decide a few days, weeks, or months after the event that they want to report it. Each state has its own statute of limitations for sexual assault, a window of time the law gives for prosecuting the crime. The time ranges from three years to no limit. If you decide some time after the fact to report it, you will be glad the evidence was saved. However, hospitals don't always save the evidence for as long as the law gives you to use it.

Even though the FBI ranks rape as the second most violent crime (after murder), more than half of all rape victims do not report the assault to the police. Even fewer victims of child abuse and other forms of sexual violence report what happened to them. Some are afraid the offender or his friends will do something to get back at them if they name names. Some think—wrongly!—that they were to blame. Many just don't want to talk about something so awful and so personal. But reporting the crime is the best way to keep the perpetrator from doing it again.

Reporting the crime and pressing charges are two different things. The district attorney may choose to prosecute the rapist even if you don't press charges, especially if he has attacked other women. Usually, however, if you don't want to officially accuse him, the police and the district attorney drop the matter.

If you do press charges, two things can happen: a trial will be held or the attacker will admit what he did. If convicted, he may serve one or many more years in prison. Many cases end in plea agreements: the offender pleads guilty in return for a light sentence. If the case goes to trial, you will testify as a witness. A number of agencies provide counselors who can help you prepare for the trial and support you during it. Even though a trial may be emotionally difficult, standing up to the person who abused you can also be very empowering. It can be one step in regaining control of your life.

# Regaining Control

Regaining control of your life will take time. You have to heal emotionally as well as physically. You have to take back everything the assaulter took from you: your feeling of worth; your trust in people; your ability to do normal things like sleeping, thinking, and eating properly. You may have to overcome PTSD or a new habit of drug or alcohol abuse. Taking your life back can be a long and slow process, maybe requiring years. But you can do it.

There are people who will help you do it. You may want to be alone, but you need people around you. They may not understand everything you are feeling, but they can help you think straight and keep you involved in healthy activities. They can point out the progress you are making and remind you that the assault was not your fault. Supportive people will not let you remain a victim.

Take advantage of resources in your community. There are about 1,300 rape crisis centers in the United States. Many offer long-term counseling as well as help immediately after an incident. You can do an online search on the Rape, Abuse and Incest National Network (RAIIN) website for services located near you. See the organizations at the end of this resource for those that focus on specific types of sexual assault.

The counselors at the help centers are often not professional therapists, but they are trained and experienced at helping people overcome the effects of sexual violence. If you need professional help, they can usually refer you. Use the crisis centers or other resources to find a support group. Listening to the experiences of others lets you know you are not alone. Sharing your story gives you a measure of control. Every time you tell it, it loses some of its power over you; you grow stronger than the assault.

Support groups are places for receiving and giving. Listening to and talking with people who have had similar experiences is not only comforting, but it can offer practical coping strategies.

Stay in a support group for as long as it is helpful. You might even consider remaining in a group after you no longer feel the need so that you can help others who are where you once were. Helping others in their healing takes you beyond being a victim who has recovered; it makes you a survivor.

# GLOSSARY

**CONSENT** To give permission or agree to something.

**CYBERSTALKING** Harassing someone over the Internet.

**EXHIBITIONISM** The act of exposing one's private parts publically or to another person for the purpose of experiencing sexual satisfaction.

**EXPLICIT** Expressed very clearly, without any question as to what is meant.

**GROOMING** The process sexual predators use to get potential victims to like and trust them so they are vulnerable to the predators' sexual advances.

**INTIMATE PARTNER** A current or former spouse or other person with whom one has been or is involved in an ongoing sexual relationship.

**LIQUID ECSTASY** Street name for gamma hydroxybutyrate (GHB), a sedative used as a date rape drug.

**MINOR** A person too young to have full legal responsibility for himself or herself, under the age at which he or she can give legal consent.

**PEDOPHILIA** A mental disorder in which a person is sexually attracted to children who have not yet reached puberty.

**PORNOGRAPHY** The depiction of sexual behavior—as a photograph, video, text, or any other form of media—for the primary purpose of arousing sexual interest.

**PREDATOR** A person who looks for victims to assault like a hunter looking for prey.

**PUBERTY** The age at which a person develops the physical ability to reproduce sexually, generally around twelve years in girls and fourteen in boys.

**ROOFIE** Common name for Rohypnol, a sedative used as a date rape drug.

**SEXTING**  Sending a sexually explicit picture or video via text messaging over a mobile phone.

**SEXUAL PENETRATION**  Placement of the penis or some other object into the vagina or anus.

**SOLICITATION**  Asking for something.

**SPECIAL K**  Street name for ketamine, a tranquilizer used as a date rape drug.

**STATUTE OF LIMITATIONS**  The law specifying the length of time for prosecuting a crime. After the time specified in the law, a person cannot be prosecuted for the crime.

**STREET NAME**  The common rather than scientifically correct term for a drug or other item.

**VOYEURISM**  The act of seeking sexual satisfaction by viewing nude or partially nude individuals.

Advocates for Youth
2000 M Street NW, Suite 750
Washington, DC 20036
(202) 419-3420
Web Site: http://www.advocatesforyouth.org/index.php
Advocates for Youth supports efforts that help young people
    make informed and responsible decisions about their
    reproductive and sexual health. It advocates for a positive
    and realistic approach to adolescent sexual health.

Break the Cycle
6029 Bristol Pkwy, Suite 201
Culver City, CA 90230
(310) 286-3383
Website: https://www.breakthecycle.org
Focusing on young people, Break the Cycle provides informa-
    tion, programs, campaigns, and education to help stop
    dating abuse and prevent unhealthy relationships.

The Canadian Women's Health Network
419 Graham Avenue, Suite 203
Winnipeg, MB R3C 0M3
Canada
(204) 942-5500
Website: http://www.cwhn.ca/en
The Canadian Women's Health Network is a national
    organization that collects, produces, and distributes
    information, resources, and ideas that improve women's
    health and lives. Its website allows a national search of rape
    crisis centers.

Childhelp
4350 E. Camelback Road, Building F250
Phoenix, AZ 85018
(480) 922-8212
Website: https://www.childhelp.org
Childhelp is a national organization that offers a child abuse
    hotline and prevention, intervention, and treatment
    programs to meet the physical, emotional, educational,
    and spiritual needs of abused, neglected, and at-risk
    children.

Loveisrespect
P.O. Box 16180
Austin, TX 78716
(866) 331-9474
Web Site: http://www.loveisrespect.org
Loveisrespect is a project of the National Domestic Violence
    Hotline and Break the Cycle. This organization provides
    resources to engage, educate, and empower youth and
    young adults to prevent and end abusive relationships.

National Center for Missing and Exploited Children
Charles B. Wang International Children's Building
699 Prince Street
Alexandria, VA 22314-3175
(703) 224-2150
Website: http://www.missingkids.com/home
24-hour call center: 1-800-THE-LOST (1-800-843-5678)
The National Center for Missing and Exploited Children is a
    nonprofit organization that works with law enforcement
    and other agencies to find missing children and provide

practical help and information on issues relating to missing and sexually exploited children. It serves as the national clearinghouse for such issues.

Rape, Abuse and Incest National Network (RAINN)
1220 L Street NW, Suite 505
Washington, DC 20005
(202) 544-3064
Website: https://rainn.org
RAINN is the largest U.S. national anti–sexual violence organization. In addition to providing a wealth of information, programs, and speakers, it partners with rape crisis centers to give victims access to local help.

Stalking Resource Center
2000 M Street NW, Suite 480
Washington, DC 20036
(202) 467-8700
Website: http://www.victimsofcrime.org/our-programs/ stalking-resource-center
A program of the National Center for Victims of Crime, the Stalking Resource Center provides information and resources regarding stalking, including details of laws, help in safety planning, and a directory of local service providers.

Victims of Violence
340 - 117 Centrepointe Drive
Ottawa, ON K2G 5X3
Canada

(613) 233-0052

Website: http://www.victimsofviolence.on.ca

Victims of Violence is a charitable organization that provides
guidance and support to victims of violent crimes and their
families, and conducts research and provides resources on
issues affecting victims of violence.

# Hotlines

For incidents or suspicions of sexual exploitation:

CyberTipline: http://www.cybertipline.com

For missing and sexually exploited children: 1-800-THE-LOST
(1-800-843-5678)

National sexual assault hotline: 1-800-656-HOPE
(1-800-656-4673)

National teen dating abuse hotline: 1-866-331-9474

National Child Abuse Hotline: 1-800-4A-CHILD
(1-800-422-4453)

Canada domestic violence hotline: 1-800-363-9010

An online message board that supports sexual assault and
sexual abuse survivors: http://www.aftersilence.org

# Websites

Because of the changing nature of Internet links, Rosen Publishing
has developed an online list of websites related to the subject of
this book. This site is updated regularly. Please use this link to
access the list:

http://www.rosenlinks.com/CVAW/Abuse

# FOR FURTHER READING

Anderson, Laurie Halse. *Speak*. New York, NY: Farrar, Straus, and Giroux, 1999.

Atkinson, Matt. *Letters from Survivors: Words of Comfort for Women Recovering from Rape*. Oklahoma City, OK: RAR Publishing, 2010.

Bromley, Nicole Braddock. *Hush: Moving from Silence to Healing After Childhood Sexual Abuse*. Chicago, IL: Moody: 2007.

Bryant-Davis, Thema, ed. *Surviving Sexual Violence: A Guide to Recovery and Empowerment*. Lanham, MD: Rowman & Littlefield, 2011.

Domitrz, Michael, ed. *Voices of Courage: Inspiration from Survivors of Sexual Abuse*. Greenfield, WI: Awareness Publications, 2005.

Fedderson, Yvonne, and Sara O'Meara. *Silence Broken: Moving from a Loss of Innocence to a World of Healing and Love*. San Diego, CA: Jodere Group, 2003.

Feuereisen, Patti. *Invisible Girls: The Truth About Sexual Abuse: A Book for Teen Girls, Young Women, and Everyone Who Cares About Them*. Berkeley, CA: Seal Press, 2005.

Gerdes, Louise I. *Teen Dating* (Opposing Viewpoints series). Farmington Hills, MI: Greenhaven Press, 2013.

Hiber, Amanda, ed. *Sexual Violence* (Opposing Viewpoints series). Farmington Hills, MI: Greenhaven Press, 2014.

Jennings, Alison. *Self Care After Sexual Assault: 10 Ways to Start Healing*. Seattle, WA: Amazon Digital Services, 2014.

Kaplan, Alisa. *Still Room for Hope: A Survivor's Story of Sexual Assault, Forgiveness, and Freedom*. Nashville, TN: FaithWords, 2015.

Lehman, Carolyn. *Strong at the Heart: How It Feels to Heal from Sexual Abuse*. New York, NY: Farrar, Straus, and Giroux, 2005.

Levy, Barrie. *In Love and in Danger: A Teen's Guide to Breaking Free of Abusive Relationships*. Berkeley, CA: Seal Press, 2006.

Mather, Cynthia. *How Long Does It Hurt? A Guide to Recovering from Incest and Sexual Abuse for Teenagers, Their Friends, and Their Families*. Rev. ed. San Francisco, CA: Jossey-Bass, 2014.

McKinnon, Marjorie. *REPAIR for Teens: A Program for Recovery from Incest & Childhood Sexual Abuse*. Ann Arbor, MI: Loving Healing Press, 2012.

Ream, Anne K. *Lived Through This: Listening to the Stories of Sexual Violence Survivors*. Boston, MA: Beacon Press, 2014.

Safe Horizon. *A Recovery Guide for Survivor*s (http://www.safehorizon.org/uploads/pdfs/1386087773_After_Sexual_Assault_Bklt.pdf).

Stephens, Aarti D., ed. *Sexual Violence* (Opposing Viewpoints series). Farmington Hills, MI: Greenhaven Press, 2012.

Wilkins, Jessica. *Straight Talk About Date Rape* (Straight Talk About...) New York, NY: Crabtree Publishing Company, 2011.

# BIBLIOGRAPHY

Allyson, Tiffany. "I Was Sexually Abused." *Christianity Today*. Retrieved November 3, 2014 (http://www.christianitytoday.com/iyf/hottopics/selfesteem/1.52.html).

American Psychological Association. "Understanding Child Sexual Abuse." December 2011. Retrieved November 4, 2014 (http://www.apa.org/pi/about/newsletter/2011/12/sexual-abuse.aspx).

Black, Michelle C., Kathleen C. Basile, Matthew J. Breiding, Sharon G. Smith, Mikel L. Walters, Melissa T. Merrick, Jieru Chen, and Mark R. Stevens. *National Intimate Partner and Sexual Violence Survey: 2010 Summary Report*. Atlanta, GA: National Center for Injury Prevention and Control, Centers for Disease Control and Prevention, 2011. Retrieved November 3, 2014 (http://www.cdc.gov/violenceprevention/pdf/nisvs_factsheet-a.pdf).

Centers for Disease Control and Prevention. "Sexual Violence: Facts at a Glance 2012." Retrieved November 3, 2014 (http://www.cdc.gov/violenceprevention/pdf/sv-datasheet-a.pdf).

Federal Bureau of Investigation. "Child Predators: Online Threat Continues to Grow." May 17, 2011. Retrieved November 5, 2014 (http://www.fbi.gov/news/stories/2011/may/predators_051711/predators_051711).

Kilpatrick, Dean G., Heidi S. Resnick, Kenneth J. Ruggiero, Lauren M. Conoscenti, and Jenna McCauley. *Drug-facilitated, Incapacitated and Forcible Rape: A National Study*. Charleston, SC: U.S. Department of Justice, 2007.

Miller, Patrick, and Alice R. Buchalter. *Internet Crimes Against Children: A Matrix of Federal and Select State Laws* (Library of Congress federal research report document 228812), 2009. Retrieved December 8, 2014 (http://www.loc.gov/rr/

frd/pdf-files/internet-report-2.pdf).

National Center for Victims of Crime. "Child Sexual Abuse
    Statistics." Retrieved November 3, 2014 (http://www.victim-
    sofcrime.org/media/reporting-on-child-sexual-abuse/
    child-sexual-abuse-statistics).

Rape, Abuse and Incest National Network. "How Often Does
    Sexual Assault Occur?" Retrieved November 3, 2014
    (https://www.rainn.org/get-information/statistics/
    frequency-of-sexual-assault).

Ream, Ann. "Survivor Stories: Sasha Walters." National Alliance
    to End Sexual Violence Voices and Faces Project. Retrieved
    November 4, 2014 (http://endsexualviolence.org/survivor-
    stories/survivor-sasha).

Snyder, Howard N. "Sexual Assault of Young Children as
    Reported to Law Enforcement: Victim, Incident, and
    Offender Characteristics." U.S. Department of Justice,
    Bureau of Justice Statistics, 2000. Retrieved November 3,
    2014 (http://www.bjs.gov/content/pub/pdf/saycrle.pdf).

Truman, J., L. Langton, and M. Planty. "Criminal Victimization
    2012." U.S. Department of Justice, Office of Justice
    Programs, Bureau of Justice Statistics, October 2013.
    Retrieved November 11, 2014 (http://www.bjs.gov/content/
    pub/pdf/cv12.pdf).

U.S. Department of Justice. "Facts and Statistics." Retrieved
    November 3, 2014 (http://www.nsopw.gov/en/Education/
    FactsStatistics#reference).

U.S. Department of Justice. "Sexual Assault." Retrieved
    November 8, 2014 (http://www.justice.gov/ovw/
    sexual-assault).

Wolak, Janis, David Finkelhor, and Kimberly Mitchell. "1 in 7
    Youth: The Statistics About Online Sexual Solicitations."

Crimes Against Children Research Center, 2007. Retrieved December 6, 2014 (http://www.unh.edu/ccrc/internet-crimes/factsheet_1in7.html).

Wolak, Janis, Kimberly Mitchell, and David Finkelhor. "Online Victimization of Youth: Five Years Later." National Center for Missing and Exploited Children, 2006. Retrieved December 6, 2014 (http://www.unh.edu/ccrc/pdf/CV138.pdf).

# P

pedophilia, 19, 26
pornography, 9, 27, 28–29
    child, 9, 19, 29, 32
    revenge porn, 32
prostitution, 19
protecting yourself, 39–40

# R

rape, 12, 34
    acquaintance/date, 34, 36, 39, 45
    statistics on, 7
    statutory, 20
Rape, Abuse, and Incest National Network (RAINN),
    7, 48
relationships, sexual violence in, 34–40
revenge porn, 32

# S

sexting, 30–32, 33
sex trafficking, 19
sexual assault and abuse
    against children, 13, 16, 17–25, 47
    definition of, 7–8, 9
    effects of, 24–25, 42–43
    electronic, 26–33
    examples of, 5–6, 22, 30, 45–46
    forms of, 7–16
    getting help/healing 6, 24–25, 41, 43–45, 48–49
    myths and facts about, 12
    protecting yourself, 39–40
    in relationships, 34–40
    reporting, 13–14, 23–24, 25, 43–45, 46–47
    serial abuse, 19
    statistics on, 7, 13
    vocabulary of child abuse, 17–19
    who the abusers are, 6, 15–16, 22, 23
sexual behavior, 8–9
    noncontact, 9
solicitations, sexual, 28

## About the Author

As a youth worker, Ann Byers began and directed a club and mentoring program for teen parents. For more than twenty years, she has worked with teens and young women encountering and recovering from a variety of types of sexual violence. She has helped and supported women as they left unhealthy situations, formed and strengthened good relationships, and healed from sexual trauma.

## Photo Credits